How Great Is God?

And Bonus

Will There Be Milkshakes In Heaven?

From the Adventures of Lazurus Lion & Club K4C

By Terrence G. Clark

How Great Is God?   Terrence G. Clark

All rights reserved. No part of this publication may be reproduced, stored in a retrieval system, or transmitted in any form or by any means—electronic, mechanical, photocopy, recording, or any other—except for brief quotation in printed reviews, without the prior permission of the publisher.

ISBN: 978-0-9889866-2-6 (paperback)
ISBN: 978-0-9889866-3-3 (ebook)

Copyright © 2012 by Terrence G. Clark
Published by: The Glory Cloud publications LLC
PO Box 193, Sicklerville NJ 08081
Theglorycloudpublications.com
Printed by Lightning Source

How Great Is God? **Terrence G. Clark**

This book is dedicated to my Cousins: Rondalyn Cooney, Regina Williams, Lynette Randall, Tina Randall and best man Lamont Johnson who have taken the journey beforehand to heaven to kick around with Jesus until the day of the Lord shall come--- see you guys then.

How Great Is God? **Terrence G. Clark**

How Great Is God?   Terrence G. Clark

Not too long ago, at Club K4C,
   Just the two of us talked, Lazurus Lion and me.
   I asked the question that day, I needed to know—
How great is God, I wondered. I knew Laz would tell me so.

These had been my questions, while swinging on the swing,
Thinking about stuff like that and a bunch of everything;

How great is God? Is He wide or is He tall?
Is He greater than spring, summer, winter or fall?

Is He greater than the mountain that stretches way up high?
Is He greater than the clouds, the sun, stars, moon and sky?
Is He greater than the ocean, who sides I cannot see?
Is he greater than a skyscraper...hmmm,
Is God greater than a tree?

I was so full of questions; Laz had no space to speak,
I had questions for days and even into next week.

I talked and I chattered, perhaps more than I ought,
I should let Laz speak, the more that I thought.
But before I was quiet, I still continued on,
I knew that my questions would soon all be gone.
How great is the Lord that the Bible talks about?

How Great Is God?   Terrence G. Clark

Is He greater than in? Is He greater than out?
Is He greater than up? Is He greater than down?
Is He greater than a circle that keeps going round?

Is God greater than crowds at the Thanksgiving Day Parade?
Is God greater than giant balloon characters someone made?
Is He greater than the waterspout I saw on my trip?
How about greater than a truck, a car, or a rocket ship?

How Great Is God?   Terrence G. Clark

Is He greater than the dinosaur I read about in a book?
Is He greater than the zoo elephant, bathing by a brook?
Is He greater than the polar bear, a whale, tiger, or giraffe?
Is He greater than a hippopotamus,
Which always makes me laugh?

Is He greater than the questions that children often share?
Questions that their teachers just listen to and stare,
Searching for answers before saying what they think,
Answers they simply do not know, then their eyes start to blink.

Lazurus did not blink that day; he knew where to begin.
He became real excited, showed a smile, then a grin.
How great is God you ask, dear friend?
He is greater than the beginning, and greater than the end.
Back before time, when the world was in the planning stages,
God held it in His hand picturing times and ages.

How Great Is God? Terrence G. Clark

He is greater than the mountain that stretches way up high.
He is greater than the clouds, the sun, stars, moon, and sky.
He is greater than the ocean who sides I cannot see.
He is greater than a skyscraper, and much greater than a tree.

He is greater than spring, summer, winter or fall
None can compare, none is wider, or as tall.
And if by your questions, you still are not sure,
I'll add extra questions, but answer many more.

He is greater than any number, even eight plus twenty zillion,
Even if you add one more, then multiply by a trillion.
And, much greater than the sand, from the bottom of the sea,
God is the great Creator who made the universe and a flea.

He is greater than the tiny world beyond the microscope;
Greater than a prayer, a wish, a dream, or a hope.
And, greater than fireworks, the light and the sound,
He is greater than the lightning when it thunders all around.
God is greater than the crowds
At the Thanksgiving Day Parade.
And much greater than the giant balloon
Characters someone made.

How Great Is God?   Terrence G. Clark

He is greater than the waterspout you saw on your trip,
Yes greater than the truck, a car, or a rocket ship.
This is the Lord that the Bible talks about.
He is greater than in, and so much greater than out.
He is greater than up; he is greater than down.
He is greater than a circle that keeps going round.

He is greater than the dinosaur pictured in a book,
And greater than the zoo elephant bathing by a brook.
God is greater than the polar bear, a whale, tiger, or giraffe,
He is so much greater than the hippopotamus,
Which always makes me laugh.

He is greater than the questions that children often share
The queries that their teachers just listen to and stare
Searching for answers before saying what they think
Answers they simply do not know
Because their eyes start to blink.

Not too long ago, at Club K4C,
Just the two of us talked, Lazurus Lion and me.
Laz answered my questions, all I thought I had,
But I thought about more, then my face became sad.

How Great Is God?   Terrence G. Clark

To hear God is greater than all, brought so much joy,
He is greater than a holiday and a Christmas toy.
He is greater than everything and a lot of stuff,
But is He greater than poverty among families
Who don't have enough?

How about the children I saw on TV,
Living in a place called Third World Country?
They didn't have much food and what they had was in a bowl.
It looked like dirty cream-of-wheat with no toast, bread or roll.

Is He greater than problems that make people lose rest?
Is God greater than a lie and when people cheat on a test?
Is He greater than arguments and angry people who fight?
And when people act ugly, can this God make it right?

How Great Is God?   Terrence G. Clark

Is greater than the hurt that blankets other lands,
Can He put a classroom where a soldier now stands,
Not just in other places, but in this country too,
Is God greater than these things and what can He do?

Is God greater than the fighting that grips the Middle East?
I saw it on the news; they said there would be peace.
And even in America, people sometimes hurt each other,
Sadly, not just their enemies, but a sister and a brother.

Is He greater than death, when someone you know dies?
Is God greater than the tears, when a sad person cries?
Is He greater than the ugly, when people say things mean?
Is God greater than any trouble that anyone has ever seen?

Is God greater than the rain, when the sky is dark and gray?
Is He greater than a flood that washed homes and towns away?
Is He greater than a tsunami, a tornado, or an earthquake?
Is God greater than a storm
Which causes trees to bend and break?

Yes, said Lazurus quickly, but his voice began to sigh.
He is greater than the tears that come when people cry.
God is greater than the ugly, when people say things mean,
He is greater than any trouble that anyone has ever seen.

God is greater than sickness, cancer, AIDS and all disease.
He is powerful, Almighty. He brings people to their knees.
He is greater than fear that tries to stwallow your breath.
And without a doubt, its true dear friend,
God is greater than death.

How Great Is God?   Terrence G. Clark

It's true; He is greater than a holiday and a Christmas toy.
God is greater than all; It is He who gives joy.
He greater than everything and a lot of stuff,
Like poverty among families who just don't have enough.

That includes the children that you see on TV,
Living in a land called Third World Country,
Where food may be scarce, just some in a bowl,
God offers so much more than cream-of-wheat,
Toast, bread or roll.

He is greater than problems that make people lose rest.
He is greater than a lie and when people cheat on their test.
God is greater than arguments among people who fight,
And when people act ugly, only God can make it right.

He is greater than the hurt that blankets other lands,
There put classrooms, churches, and lemonade stands.
Not just in those places, but in this country too.
Yes, God is greater; just watch what He will do!

How Great Is God?   Terrence G. Clark

He is much greater than the fighting that grips the Middle East.
To those who trust in His good news,
He will bring real and lasting peace.
God is faithful to the people, who faithfully invite others,
To enter into His kingdom and treat all as sisters and brothers.

He is greater than the rain, when the sky is dark and gray.
He is greater than a flood that washed homes and towns away.
He is greater than a tsunami, a tornado, or an earthquake,
He is greater than a storm,
Which causes trees to bend and break.

Then Laz lifted both hands high
And stretched them over his head.
He looked at me, nodded, smiled and then he said:
Your questions pass the ceiling
And stretch as far as China's great wall.
Yet, God is greater than all you have asked today,
He is greater than them all.

This is what I asked at Club K4C not too long ago,
It was just Laz and me talking, and I really wanted to know.

I asked Lazurus Lion to tell me now today,
Just how great is this God to whom I always pray?
I looked up to Laz, the swing was my seat.
I was eager to let him teach me,
Now that my questions were complete.

God's a great listener: He hears our call in the night.
He is powerful, said Laz. His answers bring hope and light,
While still feeding the lions, flocks and the tiniest bird.
There are thousands calling, yet every prayer is still heard.

How Great Is God? — Terrence G. Clark

With outstretched arms He loved us,
On the cross He hung and died,
To pay the cost of our sins, the whole world wide.
Then He arose from the grave, with the victory won,
To one day take us to heaven, and now to live as His son.

He is so great that heaven, from gate to pearly gate,
Can never fully hold Him, He is just that great.
His love for us is endless, His grace and mercy much more.
He lives in hearts wide open that enter through faith's door.

So now let's praise together, join along with me,
And lift holy hands up high, as free as can be.
Giving glory to our great God, in Him we can truly boast,
For He—will never leave us—Father, Son and Holy Ghost.

God is great enough to love people,
Whose hatred for Him is wrong,
Saying nasty things about Him,
When holding their anger long.

How Great Is God?   Terrence G. Clark

He still stands at their door knocking,
From their beginning to their end,
Ready to bring them to His house,
When to Him, their knees, they bend.

So then, how great is God? I put Lazurus to the task.
He said, "Not only is He greater than the things that you ask.
He is so much greater than them all,
Number one and number ten,
And a thousand gadzillion more, even if you started again."

For God so loved the world that He gave His only son,
Through a virgin named Mary that's how it was done.
He came to walk among us, from heaven up above,
To tell us of the Father and how great is His love.

Not too long ago, at Club K4C,
Just the two of us talked quietly, Lazurus Lion and me.
I was asking so many questions about—
Is God greater than that or this?
Lazurus answered them all for me, not one did he miss.

How Great Is God? Terrence G. Clark

So when you have questions
Or to you your friends implore
Take time to talk to the Lord right now,
And read this story once more.

Will There Be Milkshakes In Heaven?

From the Adventures of Lazurus Lion and ClubK4C

By Terrence G. Clark

Will There Be Milkshakes In Heaven? Terrence G. Clark

Will there be milkshakes
in heaven?

The question came
I remember so clearly
Someone asked...
James was his name

It was when I visited
The Club K4C
Oh, pardon my manners,
I am called Abigee

Club K4C is the place
Where Kids love to be
They learn of God's Word
For their whole family

James was there
Waiting eagerly for me
With his question he brought
He had been there since three.

Such questions were normal
Many kids would write in
So I smiled and looked upwards
Yes...that's where I'll begin

They'll be diamonds and rainbows
From the Scripture I read
Topaz and rubies
And more to be said

Cherry

Peach

Cherry Cheese Cake

Cherry Vanilla

Chocolate

Butter Pecan

Butter Almond

Pistachio

Blue berry

Coconut

Pineapple

Root beer

Grape

Peanut Butter

Apple Pie

Peach Pie

Will There Be Milkshakes In Heaven? — Terrence G. Clark

I know of the river	Extra Thick
It's crystal...we'll see	
You come and are healed	Apricot
Because there's the Life Tree	
	Black Cherry
With leaves for all nations	
For all who will come	
Sample twelve kinds of fruit	Vanilla Bean
Sound so good...want some?	
	Butter scotch
There is also a street	Caramel
Made of pure shining gold	
It leads to the city	Sugar cone
Of that I am told	Birthday Cake
The place is so awesome	Amaretto
It's flooded with light	
Yet, no sun shines there	Cola
No moon, no night	Bacon
There are legions of angels	Walnut
The ones that are there	
The rest have been sent	Cappuccino
To the earth they are here	Fudge
What else is in heaven?	Ginger
Of course, there's the throne	
And the One who sits on it	Gingerbread
He is God...Him alone	Toffee
He's the Great God Almighty	Peach pie
The Father of all	
And when we do see Him	Hot fudge
To the ground we will fall	Peanut Butter

Will There Be Milkshakes In Heaven?   Terrence G. Clark

We will fall in His power	Chocolate Mint
I do not know why	
But when He is near	Fudge
With joy I do cry	Maple
He has given me Jesus	Coffee
He is God's Son	
Who died on the cross	Candy Caney
My freedom He won	Butter Ripple
So I am certain He loves me	Peanut Butter Cup
No one else can love more	Mango
Because His death paid the price	
For my sins that He bore	Birthday Cake
Now James didn't wiggle	Peppermint
He just looked and he stared	Orange
I could see he was happy	
With the story I shared	Lemon
But James still had his question	Apricot
He hadn't forgot:	Butter cream
Will there be milkshakes in heaven?	
I like them a lot	Cheese Cake
If not, I still want to go there	Cherry
But I thought if there might	Unity
I could share one with Jesus	
What fun and so right	Rum
You see, sipping milkshakes with friends	Almond Coconut
Was the best that James knew	Chocolate
To share one with his Savior	
Was the best thing to do	Mint

Will There Be Milkshakes In Heaven? Terrence G. Clark

This is just a story
From me Abigee
Told many times
At Club K4C

But read the Holy Bible
To settle the facts
That heaven's a real place
So don't fear-relax

It's full of life and God's people
The ones that go there
And we'll be caught up to meet them
One day in the air

But you have to be ready
Like a milkshake that's sweet
Made right by faith in His grace
...In Him were complete

So on the way over
Before stopping here today
I went to *Shake Heaven*
There's one on the way

They make the best strawberry
Extra thick if you say
And no extra charge
It's the deal every day

I bought you vanilla
The banana's for me
Now...Let's hang out with Jesus
That's how heaven will be.
The End

Brownie

Banana

Vanilla

Egg Nog

Frozen Yogurt

Orange Sherbet

Praline

Rocky Road

Rum Raisin

Butter Brickle

Maple Nut

Pina Colada

Tea berry

Pumpkin

Fat Free

Malt

The Adventures of Lazurus Lion and ClubK4C is a periodic story published in the Voice of *One* Christian News & Commentary magazine a publication of The Glory Cloud publications.

Lazurus Lion ™ & ClubK4C ™ is a production and ministry of the of The Glory Cloud publications ™ and Terrence G. Clark.

Use of the ClubK4C name and images are prohibited without permission from The Glory Cloud publications and Terrence G. Clark.

For more information on ClubK4C, Lazurus Lion, the ClubK4C team. ClubK4C productions & publications (clothing line, comics, books, music, website), or the author Terrence G. Clark -- contact the publisher The Glory Cloud publications

The Glory Cloud publications
PO Box 193 Sicklerville NJ 08081
Theglorycloudpublication.com
Clubk4c.tv

Lazurus Lion

www.ingramcontent.com/pod-product-compliance
Lightning Source LLC
Chambersburg PA
CBHW032019290426
44109CB00013B/721